Veer, Oscillate, Rest

Veer, Oscillate, Rest

poems by

Carrie Etter

Shearsman Books

First published in the United Kingdom in 2025 by
Shearsman Books
P.O. Box 4239
Swindon   SN3 9FN

Shearsman Books Ltd Registered Office
30–31 St. James Place, Mangotsfield, Bristol BS16 9JB
(this address not for correspondence)

EU AUTHORISED REPRESENTATIVE:
Lightning Source France
1 Av. Johannes Gutenberg, 78310 Maurepas, France
Email: compliance@lightningsource.fr

www.shearsman.com

ISBN 978-1-84861-981-4

Copyright © Carrie Etter, 2025

The right of Carrie Etter to be identified as the author of this work has been asserted by her in accordance with the Copyrights, Designs and Patents Act of 1988. All rights reserved.

ACKNOWLEDGEMENTS

Thanks to the editors of the following journals, where these poems first appeared: *Boston Review, Chicago Review, Drunken Boat, English, Junction Box, The Mackinaw Review, New Letters, New Welsh Review, The North, Poetry Review, Poetry Wales, Raceme, Shearsman, Southword, Stand, Stride,* and *The Times Literary Supplement*.

'Ever Among' appeared in *The World Speaking Back…: to Denise Riley* (ed. Ágnes Lehóczky and Zoë Skoulding, Boiler House Press, 2018), and 'One for London' in *The Caught Habits of Language: An Entertainment for W.S. Graham for Him Having Reached One Hundred* (edited by Rachael Boast, Andy Ching, and Nathan Hamilton, Donut Press, 2018).

My particular thanks to Isabelle Thompson for her help with this manuscript and my community of poets and writers for their sustaining support.

for Hilda Sheehan

My America

says the expatriate

Daughter of Obama. Daughter of Trump. Daughter of a backyard strewn with the rusted shells of automobiles. Daughter with a revisionist memory. The wolf released to cull the deer. The deer. The Book of Revelations. The Song of Solomon. Hooters' all-you-can-eat wings night. An order for two Diet Cokes, easy ice, at McDonald's drive thru. The best taco truck in Los Angeles. Free baseball caps bearing brand logos for corn seed, hardware stores, a waste disposal company. Fantasy Football and Fantasy Island. The annual garlic/corn/watermelon/strawberry/pumpkin festival. Pumpkin spice from September through November. White policeman kills unarmed black man. 32 dead, 17 wounded at university shooting. Ranch dressing on the side. A trailer home park on the edge of town. Florida orange juice, Idaho potatoes, California raisins, Wisconsin cheese. The moon landing. Judy Garland. Sesame Street. This store offers rainchecks. Daughter of Malcolm X. Daughter of David Duke.

Project Cannikin

Amchitka Island, Alaska, 6 November 1971

Up goes the island! Up, up, up! We're testing a nuclear missile!

Up goes the island! And a man brought his wife and daughters to see it.

Up goes the island–twenty-five feet! Down come a thousand dead sea otters.

Down comes the island, down come cliffs, rocks, cormorants, eagles, falcons, ducks....

(crushed skulls) (ruptured lungs) (snapped spines)

Nine-year-old Emily said, 'It was kind of like a train ride.'

Fat

I saw that I was fat and walked and walked toward a desert only to find a case of (not light) beer.

Seeing oneself as fat often involves a photograph or a mirror, as one's image of oneself is rarely fat.

I opened a can of Diet Coke to feel a sense of commitment if not progress.

Not progress given that I have drunk Diet Coke for decades and detested my subservience to a multinational.

At this point you should say, 'At least it's not McDonald's,' to which I will nod in mitigated guilt.

If I am walking toward a desert let it be California.

I partook of California's glamour for thirteen years.

In the Midwest people say California so it seems to have five even six syllables as they try to keep the word on their tongues as long as possible.

I'd go back to the Midwest for a visit and listen to other people say California and reckon my good fortune.

I often felt fat in California, though usually I was thin.

Everyone in Los Angeles feels fat.

If you say California enough you will go there.

Sometimes I move through the world by way of illusion, harbouring an image of a woman with a weightless face.

Tornado

Grubsteaker's Restaurant, Fairdale, Illinois, April 2015

Sky churns grey,

and all turn to the plate-glass windows to see
grey go black—

clatter of cutlery, screech of chair feet across the diner floor—

twelve they scramble
into the basement and within a minute the eye

upon them, in cracking, crashing glass, tearing aluminium,
toppling tables—

in the eye in the roar in the throttle

below the eye and its wrath or its
two-hundred-mile-an-hour twist and hurl—

and gone. And twelve trapped beneath.
They wait in

the taste of oxygen.

Night England by Train

Swathes of black where I imagine fields, sheep.
If there's light, there's concrete.

On a platform's edge, leafless bushes scratch the air.
A pair of eyes, glimpse of orange fur.

Swish of tail.
The train begins again, charges west

toward a cold, black sea.
Come, it calls, but not to sleep.

Ever Among

> '...to converse with shades, yourself become a shadow.'
> Denise Riley, 'Listening for Lost People'

Where the sea bears the colour
of slate. To withdraw, to subdue
my teeming for. Call it an undersong.
The rabbit stilled in plain sight,
on the green: attentive to I
can't know what. Under an oak's
canopy, I try to empty. She is near,
in the rabbit's poise, in the long swathe.
I must and no, cannot.

Pursuit, Dublin

My destroying angel has the genitals
of a man and a fickle heart.
On Grafton Street the shoppers
absorb him without a shriek.

Laceless shoes, ringless fingers—
nothing to slow my gait,
though if he's manly, he's a fair wind—
I erode by grains.

The Rival

after Sylvia Plath's poem of the same title

My rival is not the moon, but it follows her.
She too glows through the night,

illuminates my skin to expose lesion and scar.
I am all flaw and yet.

And yet I look askance at the men she enthrones,
the walnuts and cherries she refills as they scoff,

all so she too might feed
on walnuts and cherries in her turn.

I find an exit and find
the moon follows me, too,

Whitmanesque in its sense of democracy,
so I raise my face,

drink a silvery light I cannot taste.

In the Wake, A Proposal

2017

In temperate, in cotton blend, in a combination of fluorescent
and natural light, I

proliferate, this petition signature posted, that direct debit paid,
out and out and out I go

to sigh too emphatically at the end of Body Pump, to hold
the spoonful of green curry

on my tongue a luscious, even lascivious moment longer,
to be inevitable

and for now, as yet, inexhaustible. To teem in spite of an
orange-skinned tyrant and

the beguiling (*£350 million more a week for the NHS!*)
promises of politicians,

I. And you.

The Reckoning

before the first Brexit deadline

Onto the table my husband empties the pharmacy bag of little boxes.

The Indian woman at the off-license scans white men for swastikas.

Onto the table and into a drawer yes this is stockpiling.

On the bus home watching to see if the Spanish teenagers. The surly white driver. The Polish woman with twins.

Nodding at my shelves and supposing I have enough words to last years.

My husband the insulin-dependent. My husband my heart.

The night of the referendum, I drank at The Star and swapped insults with a man who voted Leave. If I cackled if I shrugged triumphant if I.

My husband says each box of blood testing strips is enough for ten to twelve days.

My husband I think he sees me count the boxes do the multiplication touch the fear.

David Cameron Boris Johnson Michael Gove Theresa May answer me.

A year after the referendum, an elderly Englishman heard my accent and told me to go home.

My cupboards have been full since I was fourteen, since my father. There are beans, pasta, corn, tuna, sugar, flour, oil….

When my husband goes upstairs, I open the drawer. I do the math. Then I do it again.

One for London

after W.S. Graham

Language, let's traipse.
I am in milk-grey London
with white wine and a fine mood.
Though I put my back to it,

the jazz is coming for me.
Language, I'm going to need you
shortly, if I'm going to sustain
the moment's teeming.

The saxophone slithers behind
the double bass. Why name the night
when I'm in London and
wildebeest and language and wine?

Overheard in Chicago

"I'm not narcissistic. I'm not bipolar."
I have a sister who's both, but have
Four siblings and you can have expectations

Of betrayal, jealousy and one changing friend.
Rain and snow precipitate self-loathing,
A kind of self-love, perhaps. I'm not bipolar.

I have four sisters: Fate, Hope,
Death and Pandora. You can imagine
My expectations, illegitimate as I am.

Just drive two hours south to find
The lot, well settled in the Town of Normal.
Let's not talk about the weather.

Veer, Oscillate, Rest

Content: as in a feeling.
The texture of the fish
against my tongue left me *content*.

And thus transitory.
Here, some information on
the lifespan of fireflies.

What about turtles?
I know them
by their shells.

Content is mind's own weather.
Don't get me started on
my leopard-print umbrella.

If one can take a sentence for a walk, how does it work in a loop, the widely favoured form of peregrination: does the sentence end with the same word with which it began or somehow end just before it, so the first word can be touched with an outstretched hand? The loop goes down the road, up the slope, to the right past the green, along a further, flatter right through poplars and the occasional skitter of dogs, down further right into the turn, over a mud path that in summer is banked with blackberries and offers a view of sheep on the far hill. The sentence can cover a lot of ground. In the distance, looming, the wonderful If.

The sentence declares it's a cold day in early March, the maple and sycamore leafless, the daffodils tawdry with yellow. Proffer or promise. There's a reckoning of days, an interminable catalogue, a diminishment by number. Such small rooms know little oxygen. *Heave ho*, says the old man walking his little dog. *Heave ho*.

There's a kind of sentence that behaves like a cartoon mouse, excitable, cunning, gaily leading me to a cliff's edge obscured by a false backdrop. What does it want from me? The sentence will outsmart me by leading where I hadn't intended to go and exposing my gullibility. Here I am at the off license among the many flavours of potato crisps, considering the merits of sweet chilli or honey ham, when I had struck out for the open air, the blackthorn and wild garlic blooming, all the white blossoms of April. *You simply need some provisions for your walk,* the sentence says, even as I see it turn to an unseen audience and wink.

Apollo 13

'Okay, Houston, we've had a problem here.'
Jack Swigert

Jim and Jack and Fred were going to the moon, but boom! one little explosion and there go the oxygen tanks. Who can turn a lunar module into a lifeboat? They can! Yes, it is very cold, and they are so tired and thirsty, and there's not much air, but the photos of their sweethearts have to be answered. Have you even heard of a carbon dioxide scrubber? When you're almost a quarter of a million miles away from home, you'll be glad you have! The moon—O moon!—just had to wait.

Geologic

Old stone, transplant
from lakeside mountain to
pub décor, tell me an old story—

such and such a winter, such
a decade, a millennium....

Those ravages—
nuanced by numbers—
the wind's speed, inches of snowfall—

how now in the warm,
in the small?

Cordis Mundi

for Jinny Fisher

The whir of water in the radiators: winter is coming. From my window I watch the hawthorn branches, heavy with dark orange berries, bob in the wind. *Cordis Mundi*, they call this place. How many hearts, how many worlds. The cloudcover is so complete this morning the sky has become grey-white, and only with long looking do a single cloud's contours become perceptible. A gust rouses the leaves of ivy to flapping, forced applause. I'm going out—I mean, I'm going in.

Seasonal

After five in February, yet not night, not yet—
I lean into the view of my unkempt garden
and discern buds—no, tiny green flames—
on the magnolia's upstretched branches.

I lean away from winter, that halitotic uncle
lingering past his welcome, as if he was.
If he sees a bottle on the rack, he'll have
one brimful glass then another of heavy red,

and you know me—I join him. But not now.
Now I cling to the lengthening light—
I will the magnolia to bloom.

The Wood

The light wholly diffused, trunk and leaf just visible

Sound in distant recess, rustle and click and a faint whine

The floor with its sparse grasses, protruding roots, unseen life

Even the sound of breath seems apart, a part of another's

The dim enclosure of wood mistaken briefly for haven

But nowhere, distinct, self teems, grief inseparable

And now closer—cicada, cricket, squirrel, firefly—

Forest becoming as much noise as dark, presence as absence

The sorrow is like the forest floor, no one's and everyone's

The Receipts

oh and again with the receipts   *marjoram mango cauliflower*   totted up
with prices, because everything, *everything*, costs   but I prefer not to
calculate #metoo in financial terms   and the receipts suggest recipes—
surely there's a curry here?   one by one each taste   each sensory memory
the office accountant's hands on my   I first tasted curry in Los Angeles
discovered bliss in coconut milk   I was so poor I recorded each expense
somebody else must have   who bought me the Thai curry   I was down
to 32 cents one dinnertime   bought two cobs of corn   the poverty
of youth, of beginnings   reckoning not yet even   a word in my head

Moment without Momentum

Her hands smell of chopped potatoes, of earth. A quickening, even here. The sky darkens predictably. Memory alongside experience, their intricate exchange. Leeks but not onions because he. No bother. An itch, a scratch. Some amazing circuitry. The stock simmers as the ordinary continues. One beat, two—and deepens with texture. *Manifold honey.* This may be stronger than bliss. Earlier she gazed over the valley.

The Teeming

When I, adrift, find
myself in the melismatic,

the indwelling not unlike
Yeats's bee-loud glade, I

can be a body and hover,
at once. You must know

such delectable, the wet bite
of ripe plum or cherry,

the perspiring weight of
a fond gaze. This is

that, the journey of
going nowhere, oh so!

This is self on
the front burner, mind, hips

in the shimmy of
atomic perfection.

Put pumpkin seeds
in the hot skillet and hear 'em

pop: give me one
sun-glazed or rain-thick

lone loiter and I too
I am I am I am.

www.ingramcontent.com/pod-product-compliance
Lightning Source LLC
Chambersburg PA
CBHW021949040426
42448CB00008B/1308